when the

fruit falls

Paperback ISBN: 979-8-9912028-0-0
eISBN: 979-8-9912028-1-7

This book is dedicated to you; you deserve some recognition.

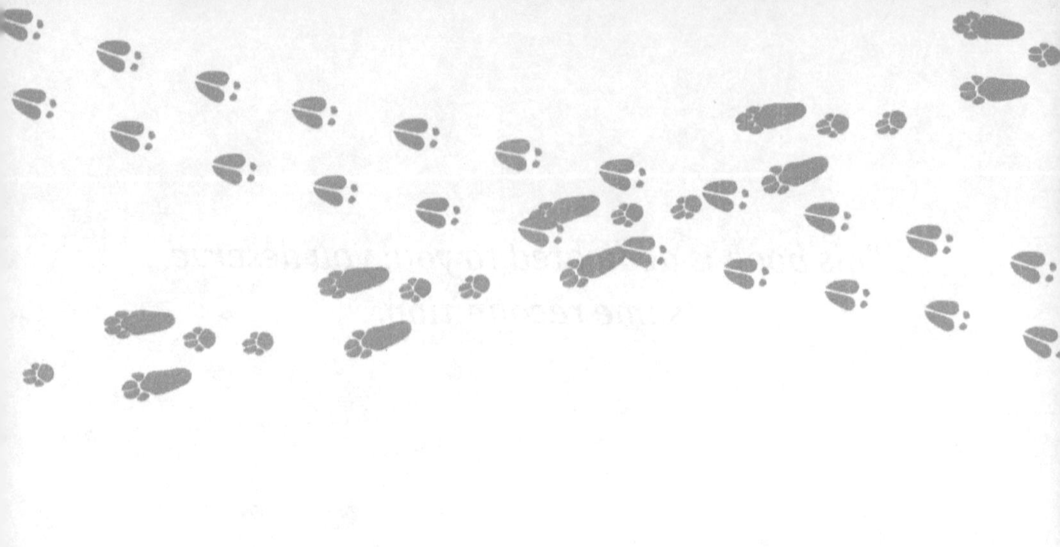

If you shake the tree, you ought to be around when the fruit falls to pick it up.

— Mary Cassatt

Table of Contents

Watermelons

Knowledge

Answers
Even the
Smartest people
On Earth
Don't know
Everything.

The distinction
Between
You and them
Is that
They know

Where to find
The answers.

Glass Ceiling
If you don't know where
The glass ceiling begins
Look for the glare,
And aim.

Share
I got lost in
The knowing.
It's lonely to glutton
And choke
On self-satisfaction.
But

No one will share it
With me.

Fighting the Rain
You can take
A fistful of rain
And throw it back
At the sky
But it will surely fall
Again.

Accept the drops
When they come.
And seek the prisms
In the sky.

You mustn't fight
The rain.

Brothers
She tethered herself to
Theory
Who embraced her warmly.
While his brother,
Practice,
Threw stones, maliciously,
Mere inches away.

He needed attention too.

Being Right
Being right in an obtuse world
Means you will look different.
You'll see the world as a spectrum
And fall in the middle
Far more often than not.
But thankfully, being so much sharper
Protects you from wide jaws of awe and
Gaping mouths which spew vitriol.
And being so much more open means
The sharpest angles intended to cut
Will swing and miss
While you're out breathing
Beautiful, clear air.
Away from extremes
And in between.

Living Nightmare
I haven't had a nightmare
In months. Maybe years?
And I was once too grateful
For the hours of restful sleep
And fruitful dreams that
Felt so much like reality
I scarcely noticed nothing scared
Me anymore. But I know a little fear
Is healthy, and it's there to help me.
If I feel no discomfort,
And I fit in my clothes,
And the fronts of my shoes
don't clash with my toes
This is surely a sign
That I haven't grown.

A living nightmare indeed.

Apples

Beauty

Shattered
When I break
I hope I shatter
All at once
And rain down
On the world
In shards of glass
Refracting lights
Into darkened corners
So the others
Can find their way
Out.

Preservation
To preserve the beauty of a flower,
She must be pressed.
From full to flat,
We only see her in two dimensions.
With her cracks and discoloration
Hidden in the back,
Or between the petals,
Lost to the eye.
Of course, she could always be dried;
Shriveled away when colors fade.
I suppose this is why I must stop
And smell the roses now.
They'll never be quite like this again.

Look
It's never been
The way you look
It's the way you look
At me.

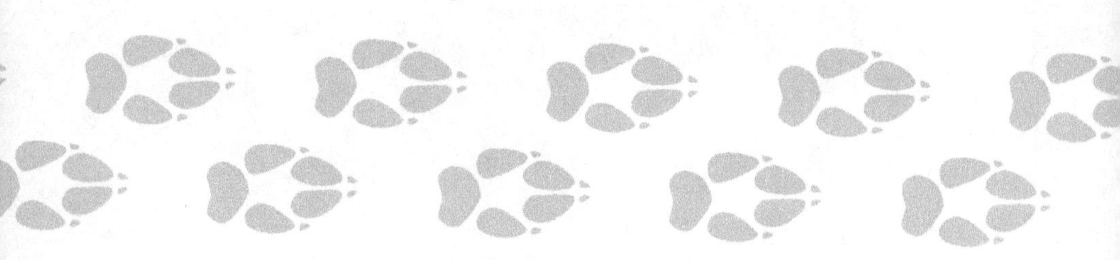

Hated
I am
Who I am
Because
I was
Who I was.

I hope
I've taken
All the hate
I've ever endured
And transformed it
Into something
Beautiful.

Inanimate
Could anything be
More beautiful
Than to have a human
Interaction with
Something inanimate?
A page or a lump of
Clay?
What is it that artists
Infuse in their work
So it might breathe
Humanity back into me?
So it can move me so
And take my own breath
Away?

Tips
He folded up his dollar
Into a beautiful butterfly.
Delicate origami are
With crisp wings
Which landed with a tap
Into our tip jar.
It was certainly the
Prettiest dollar I ever received
But I had to unfold her wings.
Even with the modifications
She was only worth
One dollar.
But even with all the modifications
She was still worth one dollar.

Mirror
I stopped saying
Others are "mean"
Or "nasty".

I started saying
Their behavior is
"Ugly."

They may not have
An ever-changing portrait
In their attic
Reflecting who they've become
On the inside.

So I'll have to be
Their mirror.

Creator
I'll tear it down
So I can take the pieces
And rebuild them
Into something better.
All you see
Is destruction,
But I see
The potential
For greatness.

Grapes

Abundance

Recompense
There is so much
The world has for me
And I could not begin
To repay it.

Sewing Seeds
I've tilled the dirt,
And buried the seeds,
I'll water and
Bathe the soil
In light until
My fingers bleed.
Somethings
Are out of my control.
Sometimes
A watched sprout
Never grows,
But I can set her
In the sun
So she can bloom
On her own.

Books and Baths
I'll take my time soaking
My mind in a hot bath
Bound in hard covers,
Dabbled with symbolism and
Metaphors and imagery,
Aromas caressing my senses
With the thrilling tingle of
Alliterations, that climax
Off my nose into falling action.
I'll overdose on beautiful
Words in beautiful books
And warm my soul with
Such a simple pleasure.

A Business
She is fruitful
That which she produces
Is of fine quality.
And while she grows
As all are apt to do,
The farmers grow greedy.
They see more and more,
So they begin to expect
They expect more and more.
Until realistic expectations
are finally not enough,

They'll uproot
Before they fertilize.
This is a business after all.
But she's still strong
And she'll grow
Wherever she's planted
With enough space and time
To expand.

Chameleon
Call me a chameleon
One eye in each direction
So I can see the world for what it is
And blend right in
I'll climb and hang,
Cling to trees
In perfect harmony
With your world.

I can be everything

Except myself.

I wouldn't even know
How to make that transition.

Aries
I whispered goodbye
To Aries
As his stars
Dove beyond
The horizon line.
And though
I mourned
His absence-

He came back.

He always does.
So keep breathing.

To Have
I hope to never
Have so much
That I forget
The first few
Things I had.

Guarantee
You can be hardest working,
The most deserving,
A waterfall of loyalty
In a forest of mangled branches
Stabbing travelers in the back at every turn.

You can be the opening to light
At the end of the tunnel
To ease someone's burdens,
But if their eyes are closed,
How can they find their way to you?

You have talent.
You may be the best.
That's no guarantee of success.

Bleed your light into the corner
That thanks you for it.

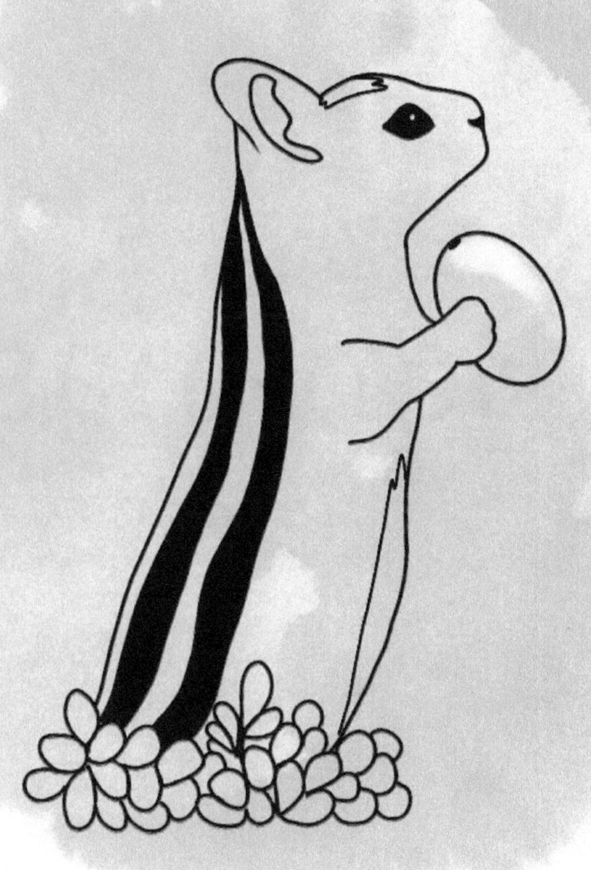

Bananas

Energy

Nervous Energy
Never gave myself time to think.
Engrossed myself in chores and
Routines to exhaust my need for
Validation from myself and
Others, so eventually I can
Unwind and finally get some
Sleep.

Stamina
Stamina only matters
In sports and academics.

Endurance keeps you
Focused longer
Running longer
Standing longer
Energized longer.

You need not be
Abused any longer.

Somethings aren't meant
To be endured.

Something New
Does spring always smell this sweet?
Or is it the end of a dark, frigid winter that
Scratches the itch behind my eyes, and
Soothes the ache in my soul to look out the
window
And see something new again.
All the fresh grass is just beyond the glass;
It's time to open the door.

Renewable
Be the wind
To push her forward;
The sun to shine
Light on her.

Avoid the waterfalls
That erode her away.
She's climbing up,
Not settling down.

Do not be finite.

She'll always deserve
More.

Fly Away
Another bird
In a cage:
I'll put all I have
Into making an escape
And flash my feathers
Until someone appreciates

All I've done for them.
That's what I deserve.

Gage and Gunpowder
Check your work and keep
A close eye on me.
Micromanage my progress
Until I fill the hole you've
So graciously manipulated me into.
Keep tamping me down
And packing me into the earth;

It'll make the explosion
So much more glorious.

You'll survive the blow,
But I'll have made my mark on you
Until you join me in the dust.

Drought
It rises in my bones
Filling up like rain gauge
Little by little until
It overflows
Evaporated by sun,
Returning in downpours
My energy comes
Just like the weather.

I cannot control
The drought.

Fuel
A tank full of spite
May run out eventually
But by then,
I'll already be flying

Pineapples

Luxury

Spoils
You were always *strong* enough
To make it,
But were you evasive enough
To avoid distraction?
Were you steady enough
To stand up to the hate?
Were you supported enough
When times got tough?

If you survived the battles,
And you answered only "yes"
In a world designed
To hinder your success

Revel in your spoils,
For you deserve it all.

Preening
If one more person
tries to clip my wings
while I'm preening,
I'm just going to
fly away.

Silly humans must
Be so jealous,
Stuck on the ground.

They lost their feathers
Long ago.

Sugar
Mother said
Sugar
Is best met
With temperance

I should have
Understood

My kindness,
Once sweet,
Has been singed
With burnout.

A caramel so thick
She no longer flows.

So now

I say,
More is only
Better
In measures
Of gratitude.

And all else
Is best met
With restraint

Unpaid Labor
I wanted to have value
To be seen as luxury.
To be revered as one-and-only
By someone or something.
I gave myself, my time, and energy
So karma would bring it back to me
And only felt more exhausted for trying

Turns out, I *am* a luxury,
I just don't work for free.

Knowledge
I don't swim
In pools
Of diamonds
And rubies
But I dive
Into knowledge;
An extravagance
So rare,
Even the wealthy
Cannot afford it.

Breathing
When did breathing
Become so indulgent?
Seems the only thing
Outside of myself
So desperately in want
Of a moment of peace
That they must rob me of it
Are my anxieties.

Deadline
The ocean of time
Is made finite
By the vessels
Her waters are trapped
Inside.

I miss when she felt
Endless
Before I got stuck
Behind the walls
Of deadlines.

Indulge
When it's been
A month of a week
Full of day-long hours,
Indulge in your dreams.
They've waited tirelessly
For you to come.

Lemons

Disappointment

Here
Don't sink so low
Into the back of your chair,
Deep into a pit
Of self-loathing,
Sagging your shoulders
Below an invisible bar.

You haven't failed yet
Because you're

Still here.

Unreleased
Disappointment
Is only
Unreleased
Anticipation.
I must squash
My expectation
And be
Spontaneously,
Pleasantly
Surprised

Gravity
Don't race down the hill so quickly.
There is no option to slow down,
And if you fall,
Gravity isn't one to show mercy.

Weights
It started simple,
A one-pound weight
I carried with ease
In my right hand.

Then,
I got bored.
I wanted more.

More weight,
A greater challenge.
I wanted to
Get stronger.

A second weight for my left,
That was easy enough to manage.

Pile it on--
Three, my elbows,
Four, my feet
Then five atop my head.

Each weight
So simple on its own
They shouldn't be a problem.

But I hadn't prepared for a
Balancing act,
I tripped, I fell
Flat.

"I thought you could handle
Some one-pound weights,
Truly, such a shame."

You thought I had such promise
Now I'm just a
Disappointment.

Better
It might not be
What you
Wanted
But
It could be

Better.

A little
Brighter.
A little more
Than what
You had.

However
Unknown,
We'll soon
Discover
What

Better

Can mean.

How Sad
Did you think I'd trip
And fall in love
With your problems?

Instead, I tripped
and spilled.

How sad that
I cannot watch you
Get on your knees

And clean the remnants
Of a cup you never filled.

Silver
If there was a prize

For being second best,
For almost making it
The most times,
For missing the target
By shooting too high.
For once,
I think I'd be the winner.

At the Top
I'm tired of wondering
What I can claim to be
A part of my identity
If I am not the best.

If you're not world champion
Do you not play chess?
If you're in the ensemble,
Aren't you still an actress?

I want to be proud of what I've done
And not feel bitter for that which I've not.
Who cares if I'm not at the top
As long as I'm off the ground?

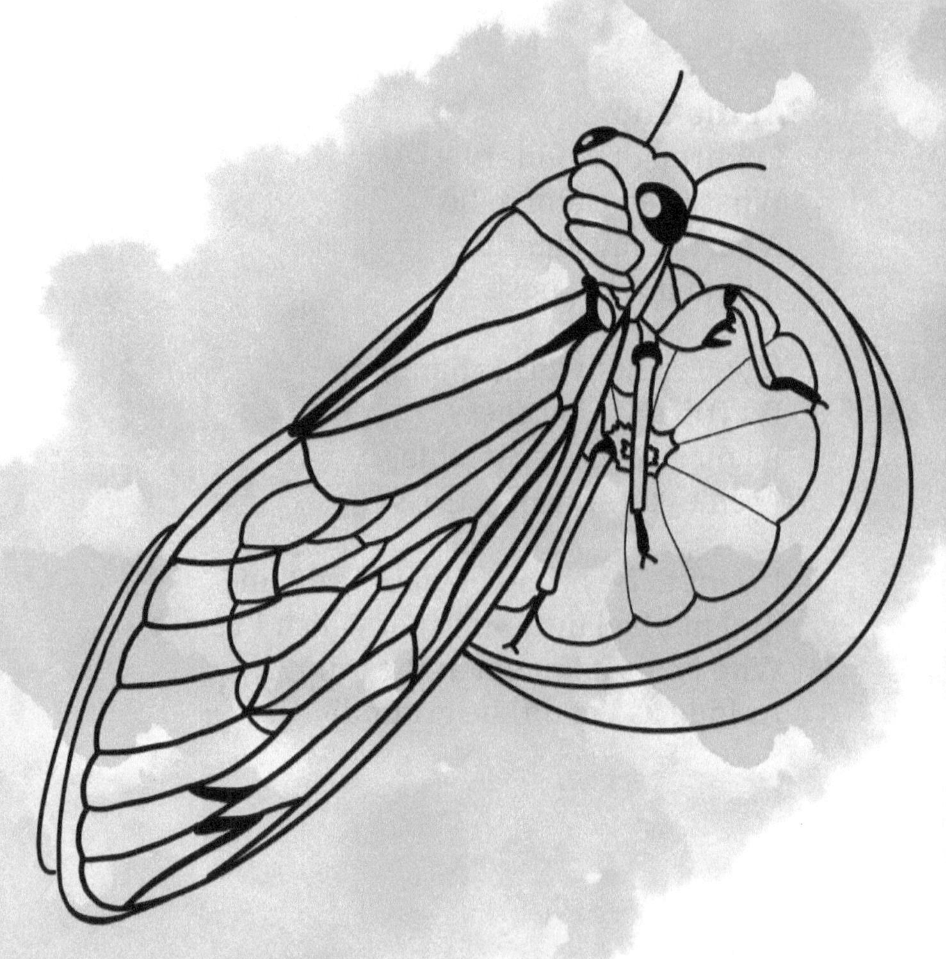

Strawberries

Perfection

Perfect
Every line
Will have a
Bend
Every color
Has to
Blend
And if it's
Perfect
In the end
Look back
And find
The lie.

Perfect
Is not
Real

Paper
Fold me,
Bend me.
That's what I do.
I'm not water.
I won't fill in the gaps.
Drop me through the slats.
And let me escape.

Pictures
She took her photos in front
Of plain, uncovered walls
So she could brush, erase
And sculpt every flaw away
With ease

And kept every adventurous
Moment captured candidly
In a folder unseen

Communicate
I can be exactly what you need.
Tell me what you want, and I'll do it.
I only need a little direction
To achieve your idea of perfection.

My World, My Everything

When your world doesn't warp in your favor
Or deign to rain mercy on you,
Get in the car and drive away.
That's not your world.
It never was.
Your world
will welcome you
With opens arms
And rock you
gently to sleep

When favor is sparse
And mercy's in drought.
When your world holds
its ground
As you ram into the
challenge
Time and
time again;
It is waiting
for you
to tire

So you sit
and submit.

Your world will
pick you back up
And hold the ram with you
To break down the walls

And let the rains grow meadows.

Cogs
The pieces
That were
Perfect
Still cannot fix
The failing cogs.

Time wore us out.

Circles

I follow the paths
Of perfect circles,
Following friends
All single file,
But they keep me
Miles from the center
And every end is
Also a start of
A new rotation
So I'll never know
What we revolve around.

I could keep on the path
Or finally know the truth.

Pressed
The perfect
Are oft punished
For being so perfect.

They are not stoned
Nor burned at the stake.

They are pressed
Under the crushing weight
Of expectations

Tangerines

Wealth

Overqualified
These aren't rejections;
They're validation.

See

Sometimes
You're overqualified
For the position
You've been wanting.

And

Not everyone has
The budget for you.

Find the ones
Who do.

Stealing
Trees don't need
To steal the leaves
From the branches
Of saplings
To feel more full.

They can grow their own.

Free
My hours
Could be
Worth millions
In memories
And knowledge
And expertise;
In savings
On moments
Of regulation,
And keeping my
Mind occupied.
I can't put
A cash value
On feeling free.

Prince
I never saw a prince
Coming to save me
From my tower.
But
I'm lucky he still
Ventured
To find me.

Lost Home
She never felt at home,
Trapped inside of brick walls
And stacking more between
Herself and her family
So her sister wouldn't see
Her losing control
And her mother wouldn't worry.
So her father wouldn't disappoint
Her with the same advice
She'd always heard.

When she spent hours after school
With friends. Holding hands and
Running wild until the night came.
And even snuggled up in bed
Wrapped in blankets and love
And warmth and joy,
She knew she couldn't stay.
Comfort didn't make it home.

When she spent hours in his arms
Whispering words of encouragement
And fears into each other's ears.
When he ran his fingers
Along her back
And stroked her hair
When she swore she'd
rather be nowhere else
But there, with him.
She still wasn't at home.

She cannot hate herself
And still feel like she's where
She needs to be.

Privilege
Privilege is opulent.
To say it does not exist
Is equivalent to pontificating on
Why they do not just eat cake.
To lavish in it is to be selfish.
To ignore it is to be blind.
So we must use our riches
To do some good.

Charity
The big, beautiful chest
With brushed brass handles, and
Stunning wood molding on each drawer
Is just too heavy for me.

I could carry it with great difficulty
Or hire a mover to assist,
Or I could leave it behind
For another to find.

I bet I'd feel good about that.
Even with no way to hold my baggage
I resign to carry another's.
It's so much easier to give than to take.

I'm rich with advice I rarely keep.

Greed

Is it greed
Or insecurity
That keeps
The haters
Ripping away
My pride?

They believe
If they steal it
From me,
It will fill
Their own
Cups.

I won't live
Impoverished.
Lacking in
Self-love, or
Wallowing in the
Squalor of
Pity.

I'll earn
That Pride back
One hundred
Times Over.

Peaches

Youth

I Am
I am
Who I am
Because
I was
Who I was.

I hope
I've taken
All the hate
I've ever endured
And transformed it
Into something
Beautiful.

New
The fountain spouts out gallons of "new"
Until it pools around my feet.

I can scoop some up until my cup is full.
But every second, it is spurting more.

So I must pour my glass
Back into the puddle.

And I notice the old
Blends in with the new again.

Learning to Love
I'd like to apologize to my thighs
For never loving you like I loved
The rest of myself, and for all the
Years of hate and complaints
That never amounted to any change.
I was too young then to realize
How you protect my bones,
How you keep me standing tall,
And the natural way you keep me
Warm in winter, and how you cushion
The head of my love as he
Rests his head in my lap.
I shouldn't have needed a man
To show me it's okay to love
Every part of myself.

Moving
My first day
On this Earth
I traveled
Thousands of miles
Through space.
I faced every corner
Of this universe,
Expanding out and
Pushing forward
From her center
While the Earth
Twirled beneath me.
Even now,
As I stand
Perfectly still,
I know
I'm moving
Somewhere.
And every moment
I'm getting closer.

Home
Did I ruin your life
By taking you away
From nostalgic places?
Taking you somewhere
Unknown, so unsafe.
Is my world so unbearable
That you carve the days into
The walls of stone that
Cage you in
While I live in memories
Of driving down
My old brick road,
Soaking in the same
Sunlight which warmed
My cheeks for the first time
Before the world crushed me
Under its thumb?

I wish we could both feel
As we did when we were young, but
I want to be your home
Now.

Motives
I asked a boy,
"Why did you kick your friend?"
He said, "I don't know."
"Well," I sighed, "I don't know
About you, but if *I* were to kick,
It would be in order to hurt."

He stared at me.
I stared back.

"I didn't want to hurt him."
"But you did," I replied,
"So you should apologize."

He repaired his hurt with words.
And the two went back to play.
I wish we all got the same grace
We give the young to not yet
Understand ourselves

Embrace
As an infant
A mother's hug
Made all my problems
Disappear.

It doesn't work
Quite the same
These days.
But it sure
Doesn't hurt.

Wrinkles
I'd rather deal
With wrinkles and
Smile lines
Than maintain
Elasticity
And never love
Never cry
Never fume
Never laugh
Never experience
Enough.

Pomegrantes

Death

Overworked
I am the best.
We know that's true
I've earned your trust.
Battled beasts for you.

You've seen my struggle
You've seen my pain
And if I'm gone?
You'll do it again.

I know you need me
To stay alive,
But me, with you?
I'd rather die.

Ghosts
Ghosts follow children
Into the dark,
And under the bed
And in their arms.

Because the shadows are only dark
And not the absence of light.
Because the children
Don't know to fear them

Yet.

It must be so lonely
To see the world go by
Without you in it.

It must be so hard
To empathize with
The wind.

The Finish
We must stop
Racing to the end.
I don't want to be
Finished so early.

Asphyxiation
Because I'm showing up on time
I get work done, I say "I'm fine"
I always smile, never whine,
I'll keep ahead, and not behind
Meeting requests never declined,
You never recognized the signs
I'm suffocating in my own mind
And left alone to rot.

The Belly of the Whale
It's damp and dank here
Quiet, and dark and dreary
But I'm not dead yet

Boredom
I'd rather spend my hours
With every inch of the world
Racing by, and experiencing
Each sight in only a moment
Than waste away tracing
Same lines of the same
Wooden box with my eyes
Until I die of boredom.

Play Dead
Let them think your candle
Has all but burned out,
Keep an ember tucked away
Where they can't extinguish you
And revive your warmth
With those who fan your flames

Mourning
If I go,
Do not
Mourn me
Long.
I'll need
Someone
To finish
What I've
Started.

Pears

Justice

Meant to Be
I'll never know why I wasn't good enough
To be a friend when I'd been kind.
I'd offered ears, I'd offered time,
I'd offered love, and peace of mind.
I'll never know what I did wrong
Because I didn't. It might not be fair
But it was never meant to be.

Watercolor
A bubble of water
Tense on the surface
Gravitating toward its own center
Will bleed out
Making branches and streaks
In all directions
Once the brush hits.
Expanding,
Like a ripple of a stone
Landing in a river.
I implore you-- please,
Choose your colors well.

They won't stop until
They reach the edge.

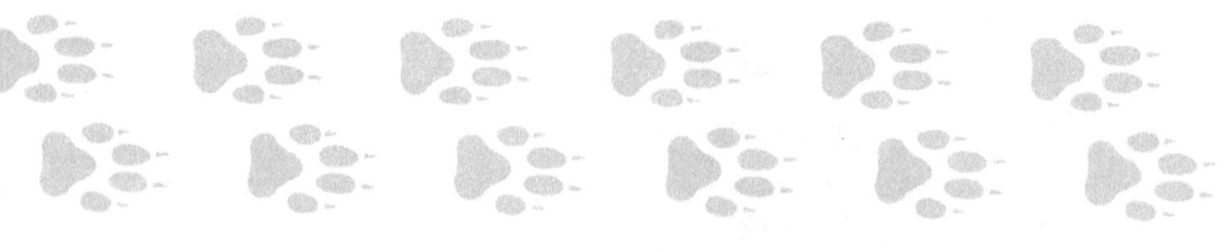

Match
You struck the match
You let it burn
You said I am to blame.
You watched it crackle.
You watched it spread.
I only fanned the flames.

Fair
It feels
Unfair
Now
But it
Will Be
Right
Again
In the
End

The Veil
It took years to find the moment when
I could make things right again

So I could make you feel the way I felt
So you might play the cards you dealt

You hung a curtain so you could hide
I pulled them promptly to the side

I slashed the holes so all would see
The nasty beast you'd surely be

You let out a deep, piercing wail;
For now, we saw you through the veil.

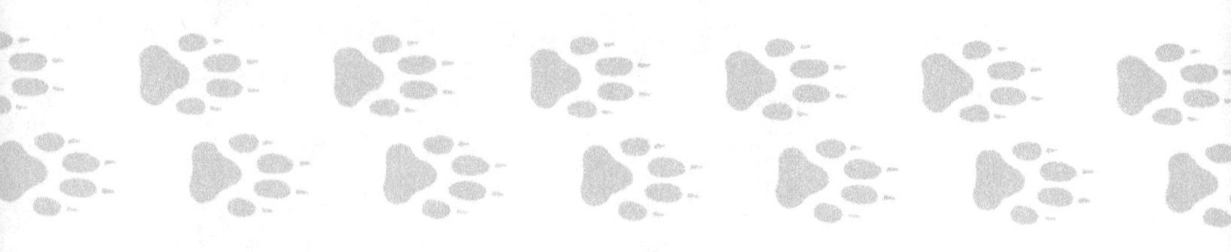

Light
Lady Justice
May cover
Her eyes
But she can still
See light.

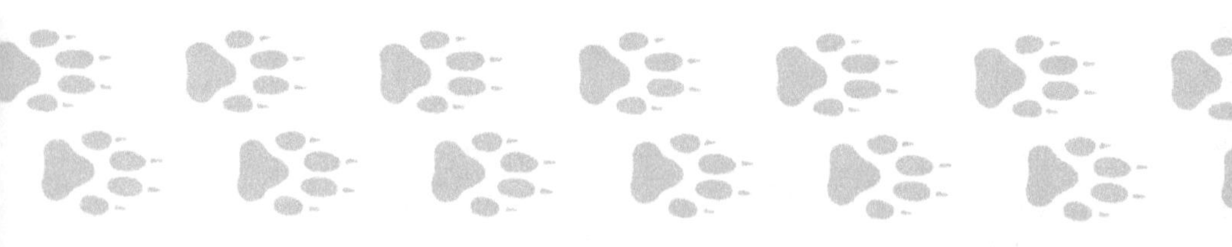

Specialization
They missed the signs
As they flew by.
They never recognized
They had jeopardized
Their lives by
Playing with mine.
Paralyzed
And terrorized,
But never realized

I specialized
In revenge.

Deserving
To be deserving
Should be no superlative.
Must I already be perfect
To deserve praise?
Must I first be suffering
In order to be saved?
Or must I simply
Fall into place?

Blackberries

Ignorance

Dark
The world won't get
Any better if you
Close your eyes
As tight as you can.
It only gets
Darker.

Learning
The only beauty
In ignorance
Is knowing
There is more
To learn

Perfume
Perfume doesn't
Mask the smell
Of a rotting soul.

Even death smells
Slightly sweet.

Proof
You said you're not
An event
In my calendar

You're a person
And this
Is a relationship

But

I'm bad at relationships
I'm forgetful
And selfish

And I want to see
A little red heart
Highlighted

In my to do list
And schedule life
Around you

To prove
My love
To you.

You are an event
But also
A priority.

I guess my proof
Was wasted
Much like my time

With you

The Whip
I've been home to many scars
You can clearly see.
And instead of going easy,
You wondered, "What's one more?"

You cracked the whip again.

You think the vulnerable are easy targets,
Well, you should have checked for scars
That haven't healed so well.
I stopped behind vulnerable years ago.

And I cracked the whip right back.

Behind the Curtain
False confidence
And ignorance
Are hard to hide
When every
Question
Becomes a
Challenge
Becomes a
Conflict
Becomes a
Failure.

I see the man
Behind the curtain

Tagging
You seem to believe
You can define my worth.
You can bend reality
To suit your fantasies.

I gave you one day
To test your judgment.
How dare you even
Put a price tag on me.

Once the sun sets,
I'll go back
To being too much
For you to afford.

Even If
I'd rather learn
All I can
Even if it's loud.
Even if it hurts.
Even if it's
Confusing, or harsh
Than only
Hear bits and pieces
Muffled through
Walls I've built
Around me,

And never

Really

Know.

Cherries

Optimism

Toxic Positivity
I could keep telling myself
Things could be worse,
Or I could do
A damn thing about it.

Optimism
Overly positive
People
Tend to
Interpret
Misgivings as isolated
Incidents, ignoring patterns
Showing one's
True colors.

Draft
Critics will read an outline
And rip open tiny holes
To fill in with dirt and grime
You will vehemently deny.
Please.
I'm still a draft.
I have revisions to go through.
You could spend hours
Stitching the meaning back
Together and dusting away
The vitriol that was pulled to
The surface. Or let it all settle
And answer the questions.
Diamonds can't be made
Without a little heat and pressure.

Focus
If I were motivated to
Sit and turn all my attention
To the beat of a butterfly's wing
I would memorize the lines
And find the words to
Describe the colors and shapes.
I could tell you how many flaps
The wings made when she landed
And remind you which way
The winds blew her.
But if you told me I must,
I'd never learn a thing.

I can focus when I want;
I only need to be ready.

Just Past Midnight
I'll keep
Watching the clock.

I don't know
when it will be
My time.

But I don't want to miss it.

Balloon
Don't fill me up
With so much hot air.
I need to follow the gales,
And I don't want to burst
Before I reach the clouds

Moths

The moth caterpillar knows on his own
To wrap himself in a cocoon
My silks may keep him warm
But they do not help him grow.

Some things must be done
On their own.

Bright Spots
I'll keep giving
My everything
To the world.
Though she
Greets me
With disdain,
I know
Nothing in
Nature is
Perfect,
But she has
Bright spots
Too.

Plums

Change

Fly

Desperate. Wriggling wildly.
I crave the sweet flavor
Of freedom on my tongue.
From blame. Or my sins.

Trapped in a silvery web
Of deception and lies,
Enshrouded in clouds of
Darkness again.

He cared for me
Or so he said,
Though now he only
Wants me dead.

He's going for the kill,
He'll eat me alive.
I'm stuck in the weaving.
I am the fly.

Spider
I spin gold into
My web
It's never felt
So much like home.

Where dust once
Settled I've
Replaced it with
Glitter and diamonds

I twisted the strands
To hold my weight
And prepare to capture
My prey.

I am the spider
And flies always come.
Now I simply sit
And wait.

Placated
I once took placation
In the form of words
Or affirmations.
Small gestures and
Pats on the head
Don't seem a fair trade
For me.

Expect a rate
Increase.

Far From the Tree
The tree
Will help
The fruit
Grow,
But once
She falls,
She's on
Her own.

Toadstools
Mushrooms wear dew drops
For a glossy shine.
A freshly clean stool for
Frogs and Toads to
Gather around and
Croak tales and songs
From years past--
Families and histories.
What could be more lovely
Than hearing how much better
The world is now?

The Home of the Chrysalis

This chrysalis teems with coiled wings.
Antennae tap at the crystalline edges
Of hard exoskeleton's translucent skin,
Tempting me with the gradients of dawn
As they give birth to the new morning.

I scratched and scraped for days to cut my
way out,
To feel the sweet breeze of freedom against
my face,
Yet I still cannot fly. My wings must dry.
I'll wait on, lest I'm torn apart by the jaws
Of fire ants, anxious to quell my urge

To fly away at last and truly come into
My true skin.
I ought to have chosen
A better place to grow
Into who I am today.

Duochrome
You can look at me
From any position
The way the light
Hits my form
May change
But I'll always stay
The same

Run
If the world
Starts to crumble
And crack
Beneath you
Recognize the signs

Take steps
In the right direction
So the earth
Doesn't sink you
In the blink of an eye.

If God gives you warning,
Hear it.
See it.
And run

Blueberries

Confidence

You Can
I'm not special.
It's only a matter of minutes,
Hours or days,
Weeks, maybe years

Before the world learns
That they can do
Everything I can do,
If not better.

And then
I remember

The difference between
Myself and others.
The thing that makes me
So amazing is that

They *could*,
But I *did*.

Voice
It's so interesting
How the voice inside my head
Which keeps me up at night
And destroys me piece by piece
Never seems to sound like me
And always rakes and
Echoes against my
Temples with the booming
Cry of every miserable man
I've ever met.

A Conversation
Do you really want this?
Of course, I do.
Why?
It makes me feel good.
But why?
Why else?

The Power of No
A "yes" to you
Isn't to please
It's because I
Believe in me.

The power is not
In "no".
It's knowing
I can say
Either.

Sharing
I'm overloaded in
Self-confidence
I write these words
As affirmations
So I can
Share the wealth.

The Sun
I refuse to be
The still water
Which reflects the
Sun's light.
I want to be
The Sun.

Take the Compliment
If I must coat you in honey
So my compliments stick,
Then that's what I must do.
I want you to wear them
Around your neck,
Up your arms,
And down your legs
So others take notice
And you
Never forget.

Ancestors
Were my ancestors known
For their greatness or wit?
Perhaps then I'll feel
I was born with my pride
Rather than fear
It is unjustified

Kiwis

Persistence

Puzzle

I've been looking for my place for so long
Like a puzzle piece, I've fallen into spaces too
wide,
Staying put, but never fully connected
Though I was never fully rejected.

I've squeezed into holes that were too tight;
I popping out at the edges, I knew I never fit
But I wanted to feel close to something for
once.

I keep trying new slots, crevices, and cavities,
Settling into openings that never feel quite
right,

Desperately seeking home.

In View
Even the natural
Stone staircase
Has a few loose
Pebbles and rocks.
But the cliff is still
In view.

Writer's Block

Should I keep writing
When I'm uninspired?

Will it read the same
Or mean the same

As the words that called
To me in the deep of night?

The ones that made me wake
To grab that pen and paper

And write before the
Perfect string of letters

And syllables slips away and
Dissolves into the gray matter

Where it might solidify
And block the neurons

As a punishment for
Ignoring their calls?

Or will persistence
Break the walls

So it will become
Inspired again?

Kicking
You let me drown
But I kept kicking.

All I need is my head
Above the water

To take one breath of
Freedom

To reset the
Timer again.

Hurdle
Stop only
Hurdling
The obstacles.
It's time to
Move them
Out of the way.

Scars
I'm no bigger,
I only climbed higher,
And I have the scars
To prove it.

You
When your identity gets wrapped
In labels and public opinion
And you're walking like a
Robot controlled by expectations
And you've been dowsed in oil
That doesn't match your make or model
It's easy to self-destruct.

Shed the robot mask, like a snake
Shake the metal loose, and molt
Into something entirely new
And entirely, truthfully, you.

The Sparkling Red
I presented the host with a bottle
Of the finest wine I could find.
Red, Rare and extravagant.
Wrapped in a beautiful bow.
Ready to be decanted and sampled.
He set a dish of crackers and cheese,
And uncorked a sparkling white.
Reds just don't go well
With these flavors.
We must wait
Until the meal is right.
My red earned a spot
On the counter,
A pretty little backdrop.
She stood out along
The wall of whites,
Making an appearance every dinner.
Making her rounds through the hands
Of the guests until she found her way
Back to her place on the shelf in
A perfectly untouched circle, surrounded
By dust and stale coffee grounds
Where she settles again,
Cemented in place.
One more trip around the room
And she'll pop before anyone
Gets taste.

Acknowledgements

I am so thrilled to be releasing book number five! Much like my second poetry collection, I started writing these pieces as I started writing my most recent novel, Never Cried Wolf. Poetry was a significant part of that book as well, which allowed me to write, not as myself, but as the characters. Suddenly I felt like I had so many ideas and I was excited to start this collection.

Then, as I wrote more, I realized there was something different about my poetry. It felt so much angrier. I'd had some pieces here and there that came from a place of sadness and frustration, but so many of these seemed to come from a place of anger. I had set goals to be uplifting and write something inspirational, and while I still hit those points in this collection in some areas, my voice didn't feel like my own anymore.

But it was. I was just feeling. And my work is not just to be read and to uplift—it is a means of catharsis for myself as well. This book was a necessary one for me because I can feel so much frustration leaving me and I also know, thanks to an incredible beta reader, that sometimes relatable is all readers need. It is validating, and this type of anger can be seen and still help someone feel less alone.

So with all that said, thank you, of course, to Kaleigh Ceci for being my thought-partner and hype-man extraordinaire! Also, a huge thank you to all my beta readers, specifically Gabrielle Dendinger and

Kaitlyn McClure, who helped guide me into the direction of a meaningful flow for this collection when I felt lost in all the words.

Thanks, as always, go to my husband, Nick, my friends, family, and all my usual supporters who go out of their way to uplift me so I can continue to do what I love to do, even when it gets hard.

You all mean the world to me, and I only wish I'll find some way to give it back to you in the future.

The next book will be a jump from anything I've done before. Who knows if I'll scrap it before I ever complete the draft, but with the amount of support I have surrounding me—I'm sure it'll come about. Until then, friends!